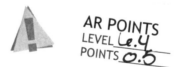

Looking at . . . Carnotaurus

A Dinosaur from the CRETACEOUS Period

THE NEW
DINOSAUR
COLLECTION

For a free color catalog describing Gareth Stevens' list of high-quality books and multimedia programs, call 1-800-542-2595 (USA) or 1-800-461-9120 (Canada). Gareth Stevens Publishing's Fax: (414) 225-0377. See our catalog, too, on the World Wide Web: http://gsinc.com

Library of Congress Cataloging-in-Publication Data

Green, Tamara, 1945-
    Looking at— Carnotaurus / by Tamara Green; illustrated
by Tony Gibbons. — North American ed.
        p. cm. — (The new dinosaur collection)
    Includes index.
    Summary: Provides information about how the carnotaurus,
a fierce crested predator living in Argentina during the Cretaceous
period, may have looked and behaved.
        ISBN 0-8368-1731-1 (lib. bdg.)
    1. Carnotaurus—Juvenile literature. [1. Carnotaurus.
2. Dinosaurus.] I. Gibbons, Tony, ill. II. Title. III. Series.
QE862.S3G745 1997
567.9'7—dc20   96-41857

This North American edition first published in 1997 by
Gareth Stevens Publishing
1555 North RiverCenter Drive, Suite 201
Milwaukee, Wisconsin 53212 USA

This U.S. edition © 1997 by Gareth Stevens, Inc. Created with original © 1996 by
Quartz Editorial Services, 112 Station Road, Edgware HA8 7AQ U.K.

Consultant: Dr. David Norman, director of the Sedgwick Museum of Geology,
University of Cambridge, England.

Additional artwork by Clare Heronneau.

Printed in the United States of America

1 2 3 4 5 6 7 8 9 01 00 99 98 97

Looking at . . . Carnotaurus

A Dinosaur from the CRETACEOUS Period

97-2061

by Tamara Green

Illustrated by Tony Gibbons

Gareth Stevens Publishing
MILWAUKEE

Contents

Introducing
Carnotaurus

Just imagine coming face-to-face with a **Carnotaurus** (<u>CAR</u>-NOH-<u>TAW</u>-_{RUS})! At first, you might not notice this curious dinosaur, since its coloring may blend in with its surroundings.

Then, suddenly, it might roar at you. As a carnivore, it could be out for the kill. Run for your life! Those strange horns it has look like powerful weapons. And it might butt you with them.

This is pure fantasy, of course, because no human beings existed in **Carnotaurus**'s time. Nor are there any **Carnotaurus** alive today. All dinosaurs are known to have become extinct about 65 million years ago.

But scientists have found out quite a bit about **Carnotaurus** from studying its skeletal remains.

We invite you to learn from their discoveries by reading on . . .

Argentinian

Carnotaurus — an Early Cretaceous dinosaur from about 140 million years ago — was a theropod whose remains were first found in Argentina, South America. Many dinosaurs belonged to this group, but they all had certain things in common. They were all carnivores with sharp teeth and claws, they all walked on two legs only, and they all had short arms. Theropods lived on Earth from about 248 million years ago when dinosaurs first evolved to when they became extinct.

But, although it was a theropod, there was also something special about **Carnotaurus**.

Look at those small, thick, bull-like horns growing over those two beady eyes! These horns gave **Carnotaurus** a completely different appearance from all other dinosaurs that paleontologists have discovered so far.

dinosaur

Smaller herbivores must have been very frightened of this dinosaur. It's because of this pair of horns that scientists gave **Carnotaurus** its name, which means "meat-eating bull."

This two-legged, meat-eating dinosaur had a fairly small, squat head; and its jaws would have been lined with lots of short but very sharp teeth. These were ideal for eating large meals of raw meat.

Carnotaurus measured about 30 feet (9 meters) from the edge of its jaw to the end of its stiff tail. That's more than the width of a single tennis court. And as you can see in this illustration, it had very knobby skin, as well as a small row of bumps all the way along its back.

Now turn the page to see what the skeleton of **Carnotaurus** was like underneath its bumpy skin covering.

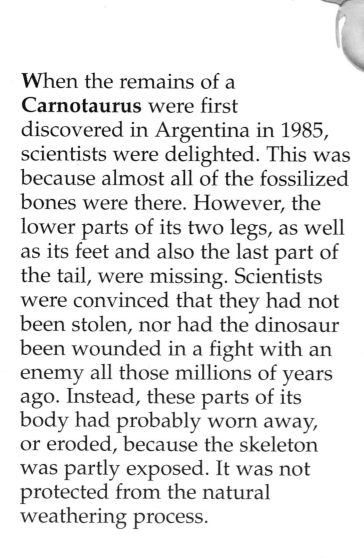

When the remains of a **Carnotaurus** were first discovered in Argentina in 1985, scientists were delighted. This was because almost all of the fossilized bones were there. However, the lower parts of its two legs, as well as its feet and also the last part of the tail, were missing. Scientists were convinced that they had not been stolen, nor had the dinosaur been wounded in a fight with an enemy all those millions of years ago. Instead, these parts of its body had probably worn away, or eroded, because the skeleton was partly exposed. It was not protected from the natural weathering process.

As a result, scientists have had to make guesses as to what certain parts of **Carnotaurus**'s body must have looked like. They can be sure, however, about its skull. Not only was it horned — although these horns were small and nothing like the size of a **Triceratops**'s (TRY-SER-A-TOPS) horns, for instance — the skull was also very short and deep.

skeleton

Scientists have estimated that **Carnotaurus**'s total body weight when it was alive and covered

By contrast, its legs were fairly long and very muscular. We do not know for sure how many toes this dinosaur had. Footprints would provide a clue, but none have been found yet. But if **Carnotaurus** was like other theropods in this respect, it probably had three clawed toes, with an extra toe-like growth that pointed backward.

Paleontologists assume that **Carnotaurus** must have been very strong; it would have fought well in battle.

with flesh would probably have been as much as one ton — that's about fifteen times heavier than today's average man.

If, sometime in the future, scientists manage to find other **Carnotaurus** skeletons that are more complete, we will be able to check whether their estimates about the missing lower legs, feet, and tail end are correct.

Now turn the page to find out more about **Carnotaurus**'s outer body. Its skin seems to have been spectacular.

9

Tough hide

When paleontologists first dug up the remains of **Carnotaurus**, there was huge excitement. Not only had they discovered an entirely new type of dinosaur, there were also impressions of its skin. Before then, only a small patch of theropod skin had ever been found.

The experts were so excited that they soon organized another expedition, hoping to discover more dinosaur skin. Looking in the same area, they found several more fossil impressions. In fact, they very soon had an excellent picture of what the skin would have looked like all over **Carnotaurus**'s body and face.

The fossil impressions show that the dinosaur's skin was very bumpy and that it was probably as tough as a rhino's hide. This would have stood up well to enemy attack, although few creatures probably dared to confront the frightening **Carnotaurus**.

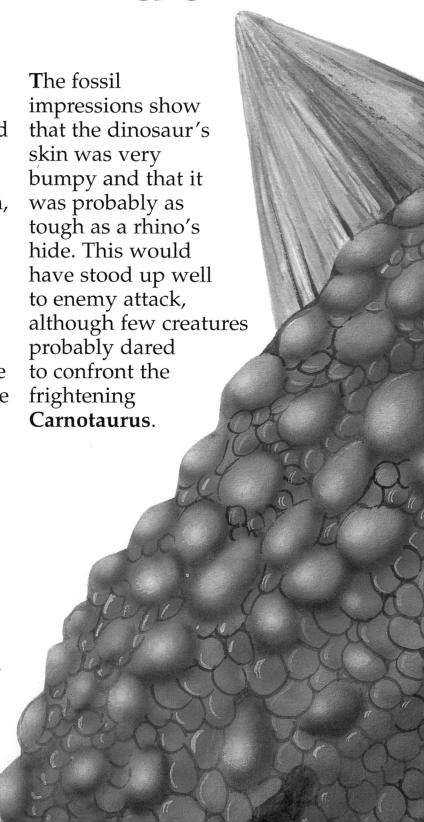

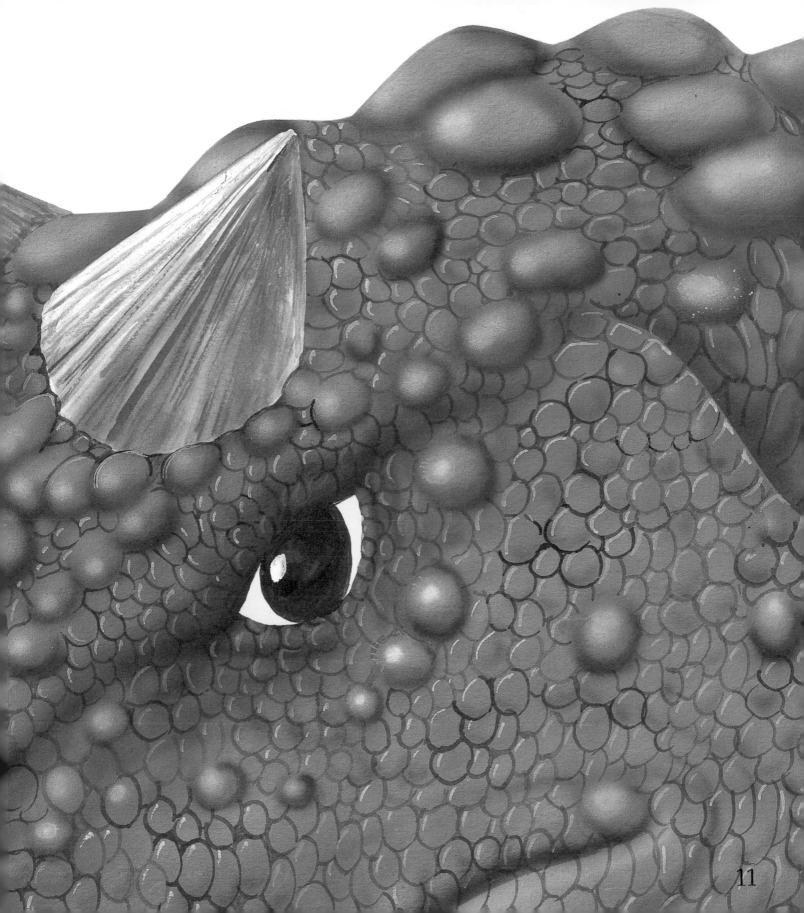

Camouflage

In his book *The Lost World* (sequel to *Jurassic Park*), author Michael Crichton describes the frightening moment when one of his characters suddenly catches sight of two large dinosaurs, standing side by side, staring at him.

Until then, the dinosaurs had been invisible, the coloring of their bodies blending in perfectly with the leaves surrounding them. (If you dressed all in green, and crawled through a field of grass, you would be perfectly camouflaged, too.)

But that's not all. In Crichton's imagination, these **Carnotaurus** could also change the color of their skin — and its patterns — in order to "disappear" in the middle of their surroundings, even more skillfully than chameleons.

No one is sure about the coloring of **Carnotaurus**, nor whether it could really change its color.

Even so, Michael Crichton's fantasy about this could have been true. And it is likely that many dinosaurs were able to camouflage themselves among the vegetation of prehistoric times — the better to hide and then jump out at a victim.

Dinosaur records

Carnotaurus might well have won a prize for being the scariest of all the dinosaurs, with its bumpy, horned face. So what other record-breaking dinosaurs do scientists know about?

First dinosaur find

The first dinosaur bone ever discovered was probably a fossil found near Oxford, England, in 1677. At first, the scientist Robert Plot thought it was an elephant bone. Then he changed his mind and said it must have belonged to a giant human being. No one knows where this fossil is today. But some experts now think it may have been the thigh bone of a **Megalosaurus** (MEG-A-LOW-SAW-RUS), a huge meat-eater that lived about 200-140 million years ago.

Toothiest dinosaurs

Once you have all *your* second teeth, there will be 32 of them. Behind their toothless beaks, the duck-billed dinosaurs, however, had lots more — as many as 480 in the upper and another 480 in the lower jaw! New teeth grew, too, if any broke. In its lifetime, a dinosaur like **Hadrosaurus** (HAD-ROW-SAW-RUS), *above*, might have grown up to 10,000 teeth!

14

Heaviest dinosaur

From the size of its skeletal remains, scientists have calculated that, when fleshed-out, **Ultrasaurus** (<u>ULL</u>-TRA-<u>SAW</u>-RUS) — another Late Jurassic dinosaur from Colorado — may have weighed as much as 55 tons. It may also have been one of the tallest dinosaurs, standing at about six times higher than an average bedroom ceiling!

Mightiest dinosaur

Built like a tank, **Ankylosaurus** (AN-<u>KY</u>-LO-<u>SAW</u>-RUS) from Late Cretaceous times had an amazing armored head and body, with reinforcement provided by several rows of nasty-looking plates and spikes. Its tail was powerful, too, ending in a bony club for swiping at enemies.

Battle of

It was a warm Cretaceous morning, and the forest was gradually coming to life. Colorful dragonflies flitted from tree to tree, and a crocodile was on the lookout for breakfast.

At the edge of the forest, a male **Carnotaurus** was feeding on a tiny **Mussaurus** (MUSS-<u>SAW</u>-RUS) that it had chased and killed as the day dawned. Suddenly, the greedy male lifted its head and sniffed the air.

It had caught sight of a female **Carnotaurus** and wanted to mate with her.

the horned

But he was not the only other **Carnotaurus** on the scene. From elsewhere in the forest, another lumbering male now appeared, roaring just as loudly. He, too, was after the female and showed that he was ready to fight off any competition for her.

Roaring again and again, one ran at the other and butted the side of its opponent's body with its small horns, knocking the rival over. The heavy dinosaur fell in a heap. It would take more than a few minutes to recover its strength and get up again.

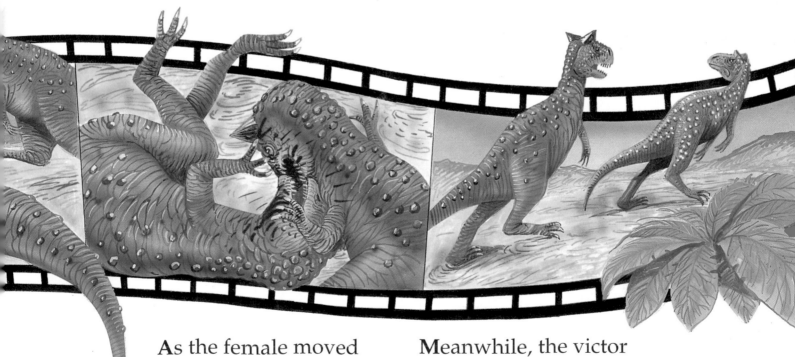

As the female moved away from the two rival males, a battle began. Ferociously, they grappled with one another in a head-to-head fight.

Meanwhile, the victor could run off to find the female over whom they had fought. She would not be far away, waiting for the male.

Cretaceous Gondwana

The world now consists of many countries divided by seas. But once it was just one great landmass, or continent, which scientists have named Pangaea (PAN-JEE-A). This meant that the first dinosaurs could wander all over Earth without having to cross any water.

Then, about 225 million years ago, the landmass gradually split into two — a northern part, called Laurasia (LOR-AYS-EE-A), and a southern part called Gondwana (GON-DWAN-A).

Carnotaurus lived about 140 million years ago in Early Cretaceous times when Gondwana began to split up. This meant that what is now Australia broke away in one great lump, together with New Zealand and also Antarctica. India broke off, and so did South America and Africa.

Because of these splits, the migration of animal life from one landmass to another gradually became less common. As a result, creatures evolving in one part of the world were often quite different from those in another.

But if a land bridge appeared as a result of a drop in sea level, animals could cross from one continent to another.

In Cretaceous Gondwana where **Carnotaurus** lived, there were forests of conifers with lush undergrowth.

18

Other dinosaurs shared the landscape of Gondwana with **Carnotaurus**. They included large, plant-eating **Titanosaurus** (TIE-TAN-OH-SAW-RUS), the sauropod in this illustration. Scientists think that, although unusual for a long-necked herbivore, the main bulk of its body was covered with knobby pieces that would have provided valuable protection against greedy predators, such as **Carnotaurus**.

The climate was warmer than it is today, but there were many rivers and streams in some areas.

19

Carnotaurus data

One of the most famous of all Argentinian dinosaur discoveries, **Carnotaurus** was unearthed in an area known as Patagonia, which is mostly grassland and desert-like areas. These **Carnotaurus** remains can be seen in the Museum of Natural Sciences in Buenos Aires, the capital of Argentina. Here are more fascinating facts about this bull-faced dinosaur.

Pointed horns

Carnotaurus is best-known for the two small but thick pointed horns that stuck out at an angle from its head. They were very effective for bashing rivals.

To this day, no other dinosaur discovered by paleontologists has had horns shaped quite like these.

Small eyes

Carnotaurus's skeletal remains show, from the size of its eye sockets, that its eyes were small. It was probably just as well — large eyes would have been easily damaged when **Carnotaurus** engaged in a horn-butting fight.

Large nostrils

Experts think **Carnotaurus** probably had big nostrils toward the front of its snout. Large nasal openings usually indicate a good sense of smell — useful for sniffing out mates or possible prey.

Slim lower jaw

Carnotaurus's lower jaw was much narrower than the upper part. Lots of slim teeth were set into both top and lower jaws. Although these teeth were not as large as those of a dinosaur like **Tyrannosaurus rex** (TIE-RAN-OH-SAW-RUS RECKS), they were still sharp. They show us that **Carnotaurus** was definitely a carnivore. (The teeth of an herbivore are usually blunt.)

Crested head

Behind its two horns, **Carnotaurus** probably had a small head crest or frill to which its jaw and neck muscles were attached. This would have made its head look even bumpier.

Smelly beast

No one really knows what **Carnotaurus** smelled like, of course, but it's not difficult to imagine! Some scientists think dinosaurs did not like water and so would not have bathed often or even at all. Their bodies were also generally so large that they could not have licked themselves clean, as cats can.

Skin impressions

Carnotaurus became well-known not only for its horns, but also because of the fossilized skin impressions that were found with its skeleton. These have given paleontologists an excellent idea of what its bumpy body covering was like. No other such superb skin fossils have been discovered yet, but scientists still hope to find more examples of the skin of other dinosaurs.

Meet the family

Carnotaurus (**1**) belongs to a family or group of dinosaurs known as the **Abelisaurids**. Most of this Cretaceous family lived in what is now South America, but some have also been found in India and Madagascar, an island off the coast of Africa in the Indian Ocean. Some scientists think that **Abelisaurids** may have existed in southern Europe, too. Let's meet a few of these two-legged, flesh-eating relatives.

Noasaurus (<u>NOH</u>-A-<u>SAW</u>-RUS) (**2**) also comes from Argentina. Its whole body was about 8 feet (2.4 m) long, and it had a very small skull. Like the rest of its family, it moved around on two strong legs. In one respect, it was different from its relatives shown here. Each foot had a sickle claw that could be raised to attack its prey or a predator. In this respect, it was similar to a **Velociraptor** (<u>VEL</u>-<u>AH</u>-SI-<u>RAP</u>-TOR).

1

2

Indosuchus (<u>IND</u>-OH-<u>SOOK</u>-US **(3)**), as its name meaning "Indian crocodile" suggests, was discovered in India in 1933. From fossils, scientists can tell that it, too, was a carnivore. Large and fearsome, it had a skull that looked like that of a **Tyrannosaurus rex**, except that **Indosuchus**'s body and teeth were smaller. Experts think it hunted ankylosaurs — plant-eating dinosaurs with armored bodies.

Abelisaurus (AB-<u>ELL</u>-EE-<u>SAW</u>-RUS) **(4)**, like **Carnotaurus**, lived in what is now Argentina. It weighed as much as 1.5 tons and was given its name, meaning "Abel's lizard," by José F. Bonaparte, the paleontologist who also named **Carnotaurus**. It is from this dinosaur that the whole family gets its name. Herbivores certainly had to be on the alert when dinosaurs of this greedy, predatory family felt it was time for a meal!

3

4

GLOSSARY

camouflage — to disguise something or someone so that it blends in with its environment.

carnivores — meat-eating animals.

conifers — woody shrubs or trees that bear their seeds in cones.

erosion — the process of being worn away a little at a time by wind, water, or other forces.

expedition — a journey or voyage.

extinct — no longer alive; dead.

fossils — traces or remains of plants and animals found in rock.

herbivores — plant-eating animals.

hide (n) — the skin of an animal.

mate (v) — to join together (animals) to produce young.

paleontologists — scientists who study the remains of plants and animals that lived millions of years ago.

predators — animals that kill other animals for food.

prey — animals that are killed for food by other animals.

remains — a skeleton, bones, or dead body.

INDEX